a

Aquariums

Wolfgang Ostermöller

Distributed in the UNITED STATES by T.F.H. Publications, Inc., 211 West
Sylvania Avenue, Neptune City, NJ 07753; in CANADA by H & L Pet Supplies
ˉInc., 27 Kingston Crescent, Kitchener, Ontario N2B 2T6; Rolf C. Hagen Ltd.,
3225 Sartelon Street, Montreal 382 Quebec; in ENGLAND by T.F.H. Publica-
tions Limited, 4 Kier Park, Ascot, Berkshire SL5 7DS; in AUSTRALIA AND
THE SOUTH PACIFIC by T.F.H. (Australia) Pty. Ltd., Box 149, Brookvale
2100 N.S.W., Australia; in NEW ZEALAND by Ross Haines & Son, Ltd., 18
Monmouth Street, Grey Lynn, Auckland 2 New Zealand; in SINGAPORE
AND MALAYSIA by MPH Distributors (S) Pte., Ltd., 601 Sims Drive,
03/07/21, Singapore 1438; in the PHILIPPINES by Bio-Research, 5 Lippay
Street, San Lorenzo Village, Makati Rizal; in SOUTH AFRICA by Multipet
Pty. Ltd., 30 Turners Avenue, Durban 4001. Published by T.F.H. Publications
Inc., Ltd. the British Crown Colony of Hong Kong.

Contents

Posters
a: Velvet-red Swordtails. Only the male has
the swordtail. Photo courtesy of Wardley Fish
Food Products.
c: Siamese Fighting Fish. Photo by Dr. Herbert R. Axelrod.
e: *Corydoras paleatus*. Photo by Hans Joachim
Richter.

A home aquarium is a thing of beauty, a family undertaking, and science lessons for the children.

Where to Put The Aquarium

For whatever reason comes to mind, the decision to buy an aquarium is quickly made. But where do we put it once we've bought it? Some, who were in a particular hurry, let themselves get so carried away by their enthusiasm that this question begins to dawn on them only when they come puffing up the stairs to their apartment with an enormous cardboard box— contents: one aquarium. Suddenly they realize this new acquisition should really have waited a bit because at the moment there is simply no suitable corner available for the tank.

The keeping of an aquarium is a hobby that is meant to inspire peace, so we should start it off quietly and with forethought. Basically, an aquarium can be put up anywhere provided we adhere to the following six fundamental rules:

1. The aquarium is not merely a container one keeps fish in; it should also be a part of the room decor. The aquarium belongs in the living room and not in the hall, the kitchen, or even the bath.

Your local pet shop or aquarium shop is the place to start your hobby.

Where to Put The Aquarium

2. We want to place the aquarium in such a way that we can comfortably observe fish and plants. This means the stand should be about 70 cm high. Your pet store can supply special aquarium stands that are just high enough to allow observation from the sofa or easy-chair, but normal tables matching the size of the tank are, of course, suitable, too. Clever home carpenters have an opportunity here to practice their skill, but when choosing the material and building the stand they have to take into consideration the weight the stand will later have to carry. A 25 gallon aquarium—not a very large tank— holds as much as two hundred pounds of water!

3. The aquarium should be standing on its permanent site from the very first day onward. Every change of site, especially where large aquaria are concerned, is extremely unpleasant. To transport a fully equipped 50-gallon tank borders on heavy labor, quite apart from the fact that a glass pane might easily break if the aquarium is knocked against something during transport. If we really cannot avoid moving the aquarium to another place, then we should take this opportunity to clean it out completely and refurnish it.

4. Set up the aquarium in such a way that the necessary servicing can

Discuss your needs with your local pet shop operator. Don't be ashamed to admit you are a beginner and have a budget. The successful aquarium shop will go out of their way to ensure that you only get peaceful, healthy fishes.

Where to Put The Aquarium

be done without difficulty. The most frequent tasks are: feeding, removal of dead animals and plants, cleaning the glass, removing silt, making water changes, and cleaning the filter. It should be possible to carry out all these operations from the front, and they should meet with no obstacles. Items of furniture do not belong in front of the aquarium, as they will inevitably be damaged by the water. Not even the most skillful worker will be able to completely prevent splashes. It would be better still if we could leave enough room at the two narrow sides to have working access from there, too. A simple aquarium is easier to look after than a built-in cabinet aquarium.

5. The aquarium should be set up as straight and as vibrationless as possible. If the floor is not quite even or the stand not level, adjust this by putting thin strips of wood or plastic underneath the stand. Aquaria that are not standing horizontally may develop a leak. If the aquarium is often made to vibrate, perhaps by very springy floorboards, then the fishes are adversely affected. With every movement conducted to the tank, they dash through the water, leap out of the tank, and might injure themselves in other ways. Under these conditions the fishes will rarely display their normal behavior patterns.

6. The aquarium must not be subjected to the full glare of the sun for the greater part of the day. Firstly, this might lead to overheating of the water and,

Where to Put The Aquarium

secondly, the plants would be stimulated to too great an activity, eventually turning the water alkaline and possibly stressing the fishes. Over and above that, many of the most beautiful aquarium plants, for example the cryptocorynes, cannot tolerate the glaring sunlight.

Naturally this rule only applies if we wish the aquarium to stand right at the window. But this site is rarely chosen because almost every aquarium has some form of artificial lighting. If for some reason you must place the tank immediately in front of the window, make sure that the upper edge of the tank does not extend beyond the window sill. Also, the tank must never be placed in front of the window in such a way that we can only look at the fishes and plants by transmitted light. Colors and shapes do not show up very well under these conditions.

Too much light has another disadvantage: the tank will be overgrown with algae. Often the algae grow to such an extreme that these unwelcome guests can barely be removed again. Here temporary covering with dark paper on the

The type of aquarium you buy may well determine the kinds of fishes you are able to keep. Your local pet shop owner should be able to show you various sizes and types of aquariums and tell you which fishes can be kept in it.

Where to Put The Aquarium

side of the tank facing the light is of help. How long and at what time of day the aquarium has to be covered depends on the angle at which the light arrives. This has to be left to your personal experience.

Two more tips with regard to setting up an aquarium in the living-room. Standing by the wall opposite the window, a sensible, simple aquarium dominates the wall and does not disturb the other furnishings of the room at all. This is one place to set up particularly large aquaria (from about 100 cm long). From the opposite window a little diffuse daylight falls on the tank and, with windows facing southeast or west, some sun also comes in from time to time, which in this case is an advantage. A

Aquariums usually require filters for aerating the water and for keeping it crystal clear. Let your aquarium shop owner discuss filters and pumps since each aquarium setup has its own requirements. Be sure you completely understand how the accessories work before you leave the store.

cupboard aquarium, set up across a corner of the room, can easily match the decorations of the room. Smaller aquaria, with a length of up to about 80 cm, look very good when arranged like this. Tastes can be argued about endlessly. It is, of course, up to the individual where in his home he would prefer to have his aquarium.

What Size and Type Aquarium?

There is only one answer to this question: as large as possible! If the space we are able to allot to our aquarium only suffices for a tank with a length of 50 cm, then we have to make do with that. But if an aquarium with a length of 80 cm fits in, that is what we set up. It is better to save up a little longer than to buy a tank that is too small. The most common and at the same time worst mistake made by beginners is the tendency to start off with a small tank until they "gain experience." They get their "experience" all right, but often of a very negative kind. Why would that be? A large aquarium is much easier to keep than a small one. One has less trouble with dirt and silt and the water remains clear, with plenty of oxygen, even if the fishes happen to be overfed at any time.

An aquarium is an environment with living conditions that are constantly changing. The fishes feed, and they excrete waste products, feces and urine, partly directly and partly only after complicated processes of conversion brought about by bacteria. Eventually the organic wastes are converted into inorganic minerals and carbon dioxide by bacteria. Inorganic mineral salts are harmless as long as they do not reach too high a concentration. The only way to counteract their accumulation is to carry out regular water changes. There is no filter that could completely remove them, and the theory that the plants in the

The first thing you must decide is how large a tank to buy. This is determined by your budget and the space available in your home. The larger the better.

What Size and Type Aquarium?

aquarium use up these minerals completely is pure myth. Even in a moderately stocked aquarium, far more nitrogen compounds occur than the plants, however luxuriant their growth, are able to take up and utilize.

In a small aquarium the harmful metabolic products naturally build up much more quickly than in a large one. Since small aquaria are often overstocked, the bacteria tend to fall behind with their decomposition work, the tank water turns into liquid manure, and fishes and plants die of autotoxification. A small tank, therefore, needs water changes much more frequently than would a large one. Very small tanks often are already overstocked with one fish. Who has not seen a tiny 1-1½ gallon aquarium where, in a turbid broth, a goldfish of 10 to 12 centimeters length spends a miserable existence?

This, of course, does not mean that small aquaria as a whole are flatly to be condemned. Small tanks are often required as quarantine tanks, for the isolation of diseased or suspected fishes, or as breeding tanks, for which they are indispensable. But the display or ornamental aquarium that is to furnish our living room for a long time should be at least 50

centimeters long, 30 centimeters broad, and 30 centimeters deep; that is, it should hold at least 10-12 gallons. Into an aquarium like that we obviously cannot put fishes that grow to too large a size and we have to be careful with the number of fishes as well.

Small aquariums are much more difficult to maintain than larger tanks since pollution takes so much less time.

But what is "large," what is "too many"? Here we apply a simple rule of thumb: the aquarium has to be ten times longer than the largest fish. In a tank that is 50 centimeters long we could thus keep fishes reaching a length of about 5 cm. Opinions vary as to the number of fishes considered permissible. We cannot base our judgment on

11

What Size and Type Aquarium?

natural conditions in this respect, for if we go by how much space and water are available to the fishes in nature, then we should not put even one guppy into a 10-gallon tank. One to two quarts of water used to be thought sufficient for a fish with a length of about 5 centimeters, but in my opinion four to five quarts can just be considered adequate. For our "model tank" this would mean a school of 10 to 15 tetras.

Apart from the capacity, the shape of our aquarium is important, too. The standard tanks offered by the pet shops are suitable for almost any purpose. Those who are not so easy to please can have their aquarium made to order or, if they are skillful enough do-it-yourselfers, even build it themselves. High-bodied and quiet fishes, like the angelfish, require tanks that are as deep as possible; fast swimming schooling fish, on the other hand, such as danios, appreciate more shallow and elongated aquaria.

Your pet shop owner can have a tank made to order, to fit any size room or corner. Octagonal, triangular, square. . .any shape is possible with all-glass construction.

What Size and Type Aquarium?

All-Glass Tanks

All-glass tanks are commonly used for both freshwater and marine fishes and are available even in very large sizes. Modern construction techniques have made glass tanks extremely reliable. They are not as delicate as they look and can be treated with as much respect as one would treat one of the old framework tanks.

One-piece tanks of glass or plastic have their uses but also have many disadvantages. Plastic scratches easily and is rapidly etched by algal colonies. Glass tanks (including goldfish bowls) are heavy, expensive for their size, delicate, and always give one a wavy, distorted view of their contents. Both types of tank can be easily cleaned and sterilized, however, so they are commonly used as breeding or rearing tanks for small fishes or as quarantine tanks.

Does the Aquarium Need a Cabinet?

"It's a matter of taste" is all one can really say to that question. If the aquarium is to be enclosed, then it has to have the appearance of a piece of furniture belonging to the decor of the room, or else it would strike one as disturbing and out of place. Conversely, a tank without a covering is simply "nothing but" an aquarium and thus always honest. It more or less automatically becomes part of the room, and our visitors can mistake it for neither an impressionistic painting nor for a bar.

What is an aquarium enclosure? What are its advantages and disadvantages? Most aquarists take an "enclosure" to be a more or less expedient conversion of the aquarium into a cabinet. If the enclosing has been done well, a display aquarium makes a better optical impression than does a "naked" aquarium that is surrounded by a chaotic jumble of all the supply leads for air, electricity, and filter. The covering can protect the aquarium from damage and it can save heating costs, but for the latter it has to be closed on all sides so that it acts like an oven. This immediately results in a disadvantage we have to struggle with: there will be condensation, and our oven becomes wet inside. Mold is but the mildest accompanying phenomenon, and what we save on electricity for the heater on the one hand is spent on insulating material on the other. So, if we do make an enclosure it is

What Size and Type Aquarium?

purely for show. We cover only the visible sides; this construction is then easier to remove again, too, than a properly fitted cabinet would be. This point matters if there is work to be done in or at the aquarium.

What is used to make the covering for the aquarium is not very important. Suitable as building materials are wood, hardboard, or chipboard. With bamboo matting, bamboo canes, or ornamental cork bark, one can transform the aquarium corner into an exotic landscape. The simplest way, however, is to buy a ready-made aquarium cabinet at the dealer's.

Our aquarium is provided with a cover not just for the impression that a "well dressed" aquarium is going to make on visitors and friends, but the cover can be made into as useful a construction item as possible. This implies that there should in every case be storage space underneath the aquarium, a disguised aquarium stand so to speak, where we can store food, nets, and breeding and quarantine tanks presently not in use. It is unbelievable how many seemingly indispensable odds and ends every

Sometimes people are so successful that their basement becomes an aquarium museum.

What Size and Type Aquarium?

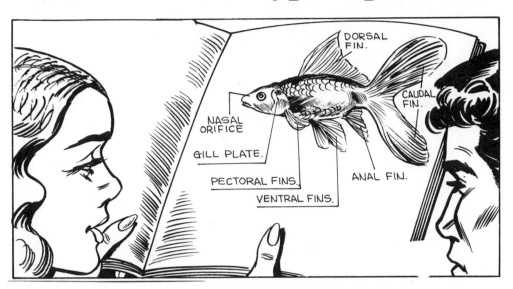

DORSAL FIN.

CAUDAL FIN.

NASAL ORIFICE

GILL PLATE.

ANAL FIN.

PECTORAL FINS.

VENTRAL FINS.

aquarist tends to gather within a short time. But we also need some space for our aquarium literature, for books and journals, that again accumulate at a rate proportional to the speed at which the beginner becomes an advanced aquarist.

There are two successful combinations that I would like to describe here:

1) The cabinet aquarium

Stand: Use a solid wood cabinet suitable for the weight of the aquarium or a metal stand into which a carpenter, or a friend who is a skilled handyman, builds a cupboard. As material, use thick plywood (8 mm) or pressboard. The cabinet and aquarium frame can be covered with a suitable wood or

You need a good aquarium book if you are going to be serious about your new hobby. Read about the best aquarium book in the world on page 80. It is called Exotic Tropical Fishes, Expanded Edition *and has over 1,300 pages!*

plastic veneer.

Aquarium: On top of this stand, put a tank that is of exactly the same length and breadth as the stand itself. Top this off with a well made reflector, make sure the aquarium is well decorated, and you have a beautiful and efficient piece of living furniture.

2) The simple aquarium

This construction consists of a wrought iron aquarium stand, without built-in cabinets, topped off by a standard aquarium. A plastic or glass plate and reflector cover the aquarium.

Outfitting the Aquarium

Such a simple and sober construction can contrast very attractively with the rest of the room and may have a better effect than the most grandiose design in Mediterranean or "Early American."

Make it a rule never to enclose breeding aquaria, since we want to ensure the best possible working access.

Dealers' tanks are usually not as decorated as home aquariums because the dealer is constantly dipping into the tank to catch fishes for sale.

If we wanted to keep nothing but fishes, we could dispense with the substrate altogether. A couple of stones or driftwood would be quite sufficient for many fishes to arrange their small living space. But who is satisfied with fishes alone? A proper aquarium should have plants, and these generally must take root in the bottom material.

Bottom Materials

Advanced aquarists not only prepare their water chemically but they also use cleverly thought-up mixtures of sand, gravel, soil, and loam for the bottom layer. But that

Captions for Color Plates
Rosy Barb, *Puntius conchonius*. Photo by H.J. Richter, p. 17. Zebra Danio, *Brachydanio rerio*. Photo by H.J. Richter, p. 18. A pair of *Capoeta tetrazona*, Tiger Barbs, spawning. Photo by H.J. Richter, p. 19. A Firemouth Cichlid, *Cichlasoma meeki*, guarding his young. Photo by H.J. Richter, pp. 20-21. A Raspberry Head Oranda Goldfish, p. 22. A Bleeding Heart Tetra, one of the few fishes that have never been spawned. Photo by H.J. Richter, p. 23. A school of Rasbora, *Rasbora heteromorpha*. Photo by H.J. Richter, p. 24.

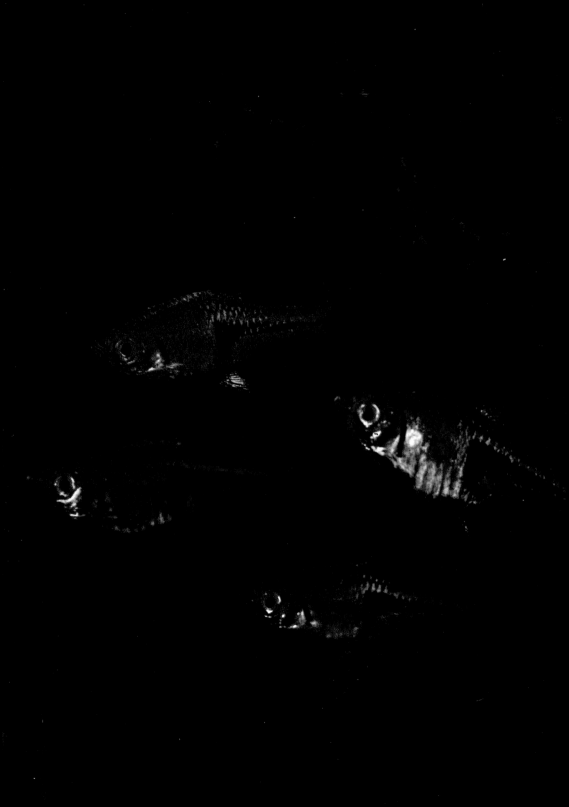

Outfitting the Aquarium

should not concern us for, as good as many of these mixtures with soil and loam may be for plant growth, they could have a harmful effect on the fishes. Play it safe and choose a mixture of sand and gravel for the bottom layer. Soil mixtures are dangerous, as they might contain a number of organic substances that decay in water and could quickly foul the whole tank.

Pure sand may be low in nutrients, but that does not matter, since after a few days or weeks the excreta of the fishes and the uneaten foods will supply sufficient nutrients—often so abundantly, in fact, that the plants are quite unable to utilize them all. More important is the question of what kind of sand should be used. The pet shops offer many varieties. There is white quartz sand in all sorts of granulations, plain sand, washed and sifted river sand, river gravel, pit sand, and, finally, even artificially colored gravel and sand.

My experience with white quartz sand and quartz gravel has not been too good. The grains reflect a lot of light and the fishes feel disturbed and never fully display their brilliant colors. Even some water plants disapprove of being illuminated from below; they decay and die. This applies above all to certain somewhat delicate cryptocoryne species. Pit sand contains too much loam and, therefore, too many nutrients.

If you don't want plants in your tank because there is no lighting available or for any other reason, you can use large stones and sand for the bottom.

Outfitting the Aquarium

The bottom layer of the aquarium should consist of river sand and river gravel. Use a mixture of all sorts of granulations, from polishing-sand size to cherry stone and chestnut size. The granulation of 0.5 to 1 mm (this is about the size of sifted river sand) should make up about three-quarters of the total bottom layer; the rest is provided by coarser granulations. This kind of bottom layer will display all sorts of color shades, is not too bright, and yet looks pleasant and natural.

We can purchase our bottom layer material at a pet shop or, if necessary, get all we need out of a brook bed ourselves. But since many of our waters are polluted and poisoned we have to be very careful.

Sometimes it is fun to have just one huge fish in your tank. That's the real way to make a fish a pet, especially if it's a cichlid.

It is safer and simpler to buy sand and gravel at the pet shop. On no account, however, must we obtain the material from a building site, for there is the danger of this sand containing additives that are harmful to fishes and plants: lime and cement, for example.

Preparing the Gravel

The bottom layer in most aquaria (Rift Lake cichlid tanks, for example, being an exception) should contain as little lime as possible, preferably none. To test its lime content is no problem. Pour some hydrochloric acid over a small sample of the bottom layer. If the acid effervesces like seltzer powder, then the sand or gravel contains a lot of lime and is unsuitable for the aquarium. If, on the other hand, no

Outfitting the Aquarium

or only very few gas bubbles appear, the mixture can be put into the aquarium. The sample contaminated with hydrochloric acid is, of course, thrown away. Quartz sand and quartz gravel are free from lime, and quartz does not affect the quality of the water in any measurable way. The disadvantages of quartz sand have already been pointed out.

No matter where the bottom material was acquired, first of all it has to be washed. To do this, take a plastic bucket with a capacity of about 2½-gallons and fill it about three-quarters full of the sand and gravel mixture. Then the mixture is rinsed thoroughly with a hose under running water. The hose must go right down to the bottom of the bucket and the water flow should be strong enough to stir up the sand but not so forceful that the sand is washed away over the brim. At the same time stir the mixture a little with the hose and your arm. At first thick clouds of fine suspended particles rise to the surface, but grow progressively less dense until eventually we get perfectly clear water running off. This takes about 10 to 15 minutes per bucket.

Sand and gravel thus washed are placed into the aquarium in

Fill a plastic bucket with sand about three-fourths full and wash it under running water. Use a hose if you have one.

handfuls. We require a layer that, sloping from the back toward the front, is about six to eight centimeters deep at the back wall of the aquarium and about three to four centimeters deep at the front wall. If preferred, the bottom layer can also be put down evenly or arranged in such a way that there is a depression in the center. This is determined above all by the arrangement of the decorations later on.

After the bottom layer has been provided, add some water to the aquarium. Then the sand and gravel will settle, but may also collapse slightly in one place or another so

Outfitting the Aquarium

that we have to remodel the aquarium. If this should cause water turbidity do not worry, for after a few days it will have disappeared completely. To begin with fill the tank only about three-quarters full of water, or preferably even slightly less.

Snails

In conjunction with this, I would like to draw your attention to a very good helper regarding the care of the bottom layer: the Malayan snail *Melanoides tuberculata.* Everybody with a small garden appreciates the

---

The inside of the aquarium should be rinsed and cleaned carefully with paper towels. No soap or detergents should be used.

earthworms that are constantly ploughing through the soil, keeping it light and loose. The earthworm of the aquarium is the Malayan snail. During the day it lives in the bottom layer and loosens it up so that no pockets full of decaying substances can build up. Owing to the snail's activity, the decaying matter deposited on the bottom layer is moved down to where it is converted by bacteria to nitrates that can be absorbed by the plants. As opposed to other aquatic snails which often cause trouble in the aquarium, this snail does not attack aquarium plants. You can purchase this useful animal quite cheaply at the pet shop or ask another aquarist to let you have a small "breeding stock." If your stock builds up too rapidly, the snails can be killed by boiling the sand or be fed to hungry snail-eating fishes, of which there are many.

Decorations

We want our aquarium to look attractive and natural. By planting it pleasantly and not stocking it with too many fishes, we have practically reached this target already. Many aquarists, however, wish to go further than that: they adorn their

Outfitting the Aquarium

tanks with stones, branches, and roots. This "decoration" can be more than a mere ornament—it can offer shelter and hiding places to shy fishes, and it can help fishes claiming a certain territory for their living space to determine the boundaries of this territory they are not prepared to share.

Aquarium decoration is a matter of taste and everyone can furnish his aquarium the way he wants it. Anybody who wishes to put a plastic toy, a small diver, or even a "garden dwarf" into his tank is welcome to do so. In my opinion, this type of "decoration" appears trashy, but if you happen to like it, go ahead! There is, however, one reservation we must make: the decoration must not be harmful to fishes or plants. There are plastic wares that discharge toxic substances into the water and thus poison the fishes. Limestone makes the water hard and alkaline, and wooden objects can foul the water if they start to rot.

I believe that stones and wood are quite sufficient as decor materials and this book shall, therefore, refrain from discussing castle ruins, garden dwarfs, ceramic divers, artificial snails, and plants made of plastic.

Stones

Stones can be found in every natural water, be it a brook, a river, a lake, or even the ocean. Hence they are the most natural decorating material. They can be put into the tank in the form of large pebbles or even built up into whole miniature rock scenes. But at all times we should only use natural stones. If you do not happen to be a geologist, you will find it somewhat difficult to decide which stones are suitable for your aquarium and which are not. Beautiful stones can be found anywhere, but the question of whether they might not give off harmful substances is not always easy to answer. We are not geologists, nor can we afford to have every stone we like examined and evaluated by a scientist. And yet there is a way for us to find out quite easily whether a stone is unsuitable for the aquarium or not.

All we need for the examination are a small bottle of hydrochloric acid and a piece of window glass. Add one drop of hydrochloric acid to the stone to be tested. If the fluid effervesces, then the stone consists of lime or at least contains lime and cannot be used for the aquarium. If the hydrochloric does not effervesce,

Outfitting the Aquarium

carry out the second test with the stone. With a pointed corner or a sharp edge of the stone, try to scratch the glass plate. If we do not succeed, then the stone is softer than glass; soft stones often contain water soluble substances. If, on the other hand, the stone is able to scratch glass, it is harder than glass and we can use it.

Thus our rule of thumb is as follows: stones that do *not* effervesce with hydrochloric acid and that scratch glass are suitable for the aquarium. This rule of thumb applies with one reservation. Strikingly colorful, strongly colored stones are best left alone, even if they scratch glass and do not cause hydrochloric acid to effervesce. For they could be ores that contain heavy metals and, therefore, be poisonous to fish.

Very suitable for the aquarium are granite, porphyry, quartz, and sandstone. Sandstone consists of quartz granules that are cemented to each other with a binding agent. If this binding agent is calcareous, the stone is unsuitable; if it is siliceous, we can put the stone into the aquarium without hesitation. The test for whether the binding agent is calcareous is again carried out with hydrochloric acid.

A few hints for the construction of the stone decoration. If one wishes to imitate the bed of a

Your pet shop owner will have lots of aquarium accessories made out of safe molded cement; many will have built-in aerators that not only enhance the looks of your aquarium but also remove harmful gases with the bubbles they release.

Outfitting the Aquarium

stream in the aquarium, distribute a few large pebbles on the bottom layer, the latter having been arranged as evenly as possible. A thin and long stone plate, slate perhaps, stuck into the bottom layer, suggests the shore. To imitate a rocky shore, pile up stones along the back wall of the aquarium. Make sure that they cannot slide and collapse. With epoxy, putty the stone arrangements in such a way that there is no danger of a "rockslide." After the adhesive has hardened, wash the whole construction thoroughly for several days, preferably in running or frequently changed water. Cement can only be recommended with reservations, and mortar should never be used—both discharge alkaline substances into the water. A rock construction should only be attempted by experienced do-it-yourself aquarists who have closely studied the many different shore types found in nature. Otherwise the design all too easily resembles a glued heap of rubble rather than natural rock. In this case it would then be much better to put only single stones into the tank, especially those that are of a naturally beautiful or bizarre shape.

A few fundamental rules for the use of stones in aquaria should be adhered to. Flat, circularly ground pebbles must never be placed upright. They should lie flat on the bottom layer. If we use slate designs, the plates should lie in a horizontal position; vertically, the arrangement would look artificial and planned. Tall rocks are never simply put down on the bottom layer. They could fall over and smash a glass pane, kill a fish, or reduce a plant to pulp. Tall stones are, therefore, embedded in the bottom layer; place them on a thin layer of sand on the bottom plate of the aquarium. Hollow spaces are straightened out with large stones. With all constructions, make sure that even burrowing fishes can neither undermine nor (of all things) transport them. Finally, we have to bear in mind that a fish might get jammed between stones if the space between the stones or between stones and aquarium wall is too narrow.

Wood

Wood almost always looks very natural and decorative in the aquarium. Ordinary woods, however, begin to rot sooner or later and foul the aquarium. They need

Outfitting the Aquarium

to be preserved or given a coat of synthetic resin—we shall leave that to advanced aquarists who are particularly keen on experimenting. We shall use only such woods as have already been preserved naturally and that, as we know from experience, do not decay even if they lie in water for decades.

In many stream beds one can find wood   roots, branches, or trunks   that have been lying buried in the bottom for many thousands of years. They are impregnated with minerals and, therefore, resist all attacks of putrefactive bacteria. It is fun to look for such petrified woods oneself, but if you do not have the opportunity to do so, you can for little money acquire petrified wood at many pet shops. Another possibility is driftwood, which comes in many bizarre shapes. Select a few attractive pieces, clean them thoroughly, and boil them for one or two hours. Usually the woods will then sink (as long as they are dry, of course, they float on the surface).

Apart from driftwood, coconut shells are another possibility. Pierce the "eyes" of a coconut to remove the milk, then halve it with a saw and take out the meat. Now the two

Driftwood and coconut shells make wonderful aquarium decorations, but they must be very clean before you put them into the tank.

halves of the shell can be used for our aquarium. With cutting pliers break a semicircular hole into each half, thus making two caves that will be welcomed as hiding places by fishes living in the bottom layers of the water. To be on the safe side, boil the cave material very thoroughly before putting it into the aquarium. The shells are heavier than water and will sink immediately.

The Back Wall

As a rule the aquarium will be standing in front of a wall. Sometimes the color or pattern on the wall detracts from the appearance of the tank. Rarely will even heavy planting be sufficient to hide the detracting colors. In this case, some type of background is necessary.

The simplest way to go about it is to paint the back wall of the aquarium with a neutral color, preferably black. But this, of course, means that the glass pane now has become a black wall once and for all. If what used to be the front window becomes scratched over the years we cannot, as is otherwise commonly done, simply turn the aquarium around and use the former

back wall as a front window. A curtain of colored cloth or paper put up behind the aquarium hides the wallpaper just as well without the aquarium itself being damaged.

We could also decorate the back wall with a veneer on which the most magnificent water plants, fishes, and sea monsters have been printed. More reasonable are the aluminized papers available in most pet shops. They come in many attractive colors and designs, and one can be found to fit any decor.

Finally, we can design our own back wall to be put up behind the aquarium and seen through the water. Onto a sheet of plywood or hardboard matching the size of the aquarium, glue decoration material such as fibrous peat or mosses, bamboo sticks, roots, and stones. The board is simply hung up or put up behind the aquarium. But if the decoration is to have a good effect the back window has to be kept clean at all times. If, on the other hand, the background is neutral, it is sufficient to clean the front window regularly, and the back window can be left to overgrow with algae.

Another possibility, of course, would be to put up such a back wall inside the aquarium. But then it takes away some of our fish's

Outfitting the Aquarium

swimming space, and we have to be very careful to choose only material that neither rots nor discharges dangerous substances into the water. The novice is strongly advised against the use of an internal back wall.

Lighting

Fishes and plants require light, oxygen, warmth, and clean water. These factors are a matter of course in nature, but we have to have technological aids to be able to provide them for our pets.

Light is of vital importance. We illuminate the aquarium not only in order to be better able to see the fishes and plants, but above all to make plant growth possible. Light that strikes the aquarium from the side is unnatural. It not only causes unnatural plant growth (plants grow towards the light) but also an unnatural posture of many fishes (the animals maintain their backs to the light even if not vertical). The light has to impinge on the aquarium from above, and that can only be achieved with artificial illumination. In practice, two sources of light are available to us: incandescent lamps and fluorescent lights.

Lighting is essential in a tank or you won't be able to see your fishes at night.

Outfitting the Aquarium

Incandescent or Fluorescent?

Incandescent lamps are cheap to purchase but use a lot of electricity and do not burn as brightly as fluorescent lamps. They get very hot and their life is relatively short. Since, over and above that, their light emission is focused, one would require several incandescent lamps for the even illumination of as large an area as possible.

Conversely, fluorescent lamps are considerably more expensive to purchase, but they consume less electricity, give off more light and less heat, and have a very long life.

Incandescent bulbs are cheaper to buy, but they give off heat and cost more to burn than fluorescent tubes.

They are also available in varying wavelengths to be used for specific purposes, such as growing plants. Because of their elongate shape, even large areas are well illuminated by them.

Arrange the lamps in such a way that most of the light falls onto the front region of the aquarium, facing the observer: then the fish also get a little light from the front. In this reflected light their colors are particularly radiant.

Fluorescent tubes are more expensive to buy and cheaper to use.

Outfitting the Aquarium

Reflectors

Reflectors must be used with either type of light for them to work most efficiently. Reflectors can also double as aquarium covers and some even have storage space for odds and ends.

An aquarium reflector sits on top of the tank. It contains either fluorescent lights or incandescent ones. You should use an aquarium cover or a full hood reflector to keep the fish from jumping and the spray from ruining the reflector.

Air

Air is required to aerate the aquarium and to operate a filter. For aeration the air is, with the aid of a pump, forced through a diffuser block of porous artificial stone or wood fitted near the bottom of the aquarium. The air bubbles then rise to the water surface and at the same time maintain the circulation of the

Outfitting the Aquarium

water. The diaphragm pump needed for air delivery technologically is an extremely simple but very reliable piece of equipment. Even a cheap diaphragm pump can operate non-stop for years without breaking down. If you have only one aquarium, then a small inexpensive pump is sufficient. But when selecting a pump, make sure that it operates as silently as possible; some types make the most nerve-shattering humming noises.

The children in the family should learn that a reflector is electrical and that it should never make contact with the aquarium water. It must never be submerged!

The air delivered by the pump is led through plastic tubes and pipes to the individual tanks. It is regulated with the aid of brass or plastic gang valves. The pump should be fitted in such a way that it stands or hangs above the water level of the aquarium. Otherwise

Your local pet shop owner can show you many different filters and aerators. All filters require pumps of some kind.

Outfitting the Aquarium

A typical outside power filter. They have been used successfully for more than 50 years.

water might be sucked into the air tube during a power shortage and then forced into the pump. If we are lucky, the pump simply ceases to operate; if we are very unlucky, the whole aquarium is emptied out and the room becomes a miniature ocean. If you cannot fit the pump

above water level, there is another possibility: Any part of the air tube connecting pump and diffuser stone or pump and filter is hung over a hook on the wall to form a sling, the highest point of which lies at least 10 centimeters above the water level. If accidentally or due to a technical fault water flows back into the air tube, it cannot go further up the tube than to the point that is as high as the water level.

Particularly densely populated aquaria and rearing containers always require aeration; it should be quite strong. A broad flow of air bubbles also produces a strong water current that ensures that the water circulates and that always different parts of the water are carried to the surface. There a gas exchange takes

An undergravel filter operates on a completely different principle than a power filter. An airlift tube sucks the water from beneath the gravel.

Outfitting the Aquarium

place; carbon dioxide is given off and oxygen taken up. Thus we achieve two things by aeration: oxygen is increased, and excessive carbon dioxide is removed. The air bubbles themselves merely rise to the surface and provide very little gas exchange.

Make sure that the air pumped into the aquarium does not contain waste gases or any other toxic substances. The pump should not be standing in a room where people are constantly smoking.

Before you buy any pump, listen to it run. Some can be very noisy and annoying.

The filter insures clean water. Aquarium filters are available in an immense number of different types and it is quite impossible to discuss these here. For our aquarium an air-driven mechanical filter is quite sufficient; it can be an internal filter fitted inside the aquarium or an external filter that is put beside the aquarium or clipped onto the frame. Both filters operate according to much the same principle.

One type of internal filter consists of a container filled with filter material and put inside the aquarium. A rising tube into which air is introduced from below is connected to the filter pot. The air bubbles going up the rising tube carry water with them and thus suck dirty water through the filter material. The purified water is pushed out again at the top. A second type of internal filter is the undergravel filter. This is placed on the bottom of the aquarium with a space underneath. The aquarium gravel, etc., is placed on top of it. Water is drawn through the gravel, through slots in the filter, and into the space below. It is then returned to the aquarium through plastic tubes.

The external filter is a filter box installed outside the aquarium in such a way that the upper edges of the two containers are about on the same level. A tube, bent to form a "U", connects the aquarium and filter according to the siphon

Outfitting the Aquarium

principle. Non-purified aquarium water flows into the filter and, as with the internal filter, is transported back into the aquarium with a filter pump after it has flowed through the filter material.

It is much more important to clean the filter material regularly than to worry about what filter type to use. What use are the biggest possible filters if we do not clean them? The dirt trapped by the filter is still within the cycle of the aquarium water. Much of it decomposes through the action of the biological filter, but some of the products of decomposition are soluble and are returned to the water. No matter how large a filter

The use of filters and aerators more than doubles the number of fishes that can be kept in your aquarium. Multiple outlets are controlled by air valves (lower illustration).

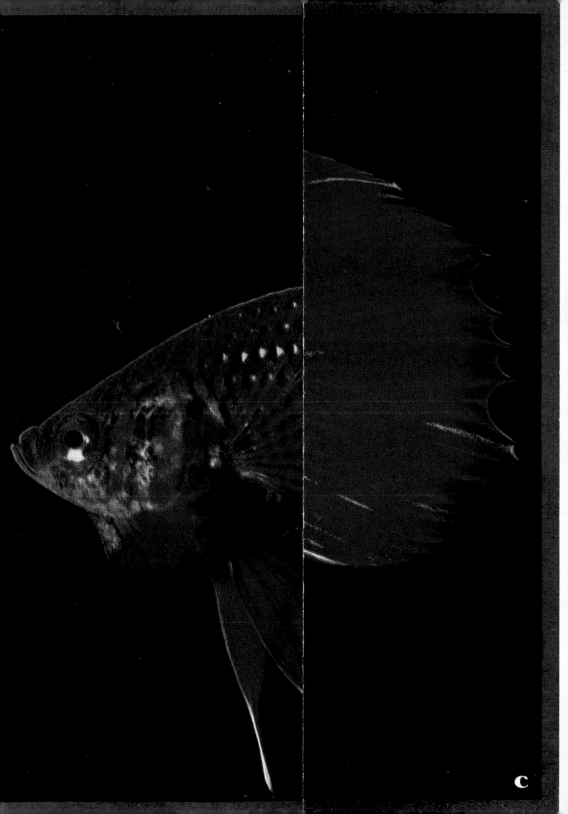

c

Outfitting the Aquarium

may be, it cannot deal with overcrowded conditions and overfeeding. Even the best of filters must be cleaned periodically.

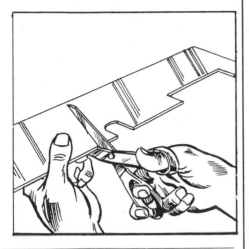

Your aquarium cover should be easy to cut so you can accommodate filter tubes, air lines, and heater tubes.

Heating

The aquarium is heated with an electric heater, a glass tube containing a coiled filament. The capacity of the heater has to be adapted to the size of the tank. Rule of thumb: one watt per quart. Today, the heater is generally combined with an automatic thermostat, so the wattage can be raised slightly. Thus we can equip a 25-gallon aquarium with a heater of 150 watts. Heater and regulator are

often combined in one instrument with only one lead wire (usually the jumble of leads and air tubes behind the aquarium is enough of a nuisance already). But purchasing thermostat and heater separately has its advantages, too: the heaters of several aquaria can be controlled with one thermostat; thermostat and heater can be fitted in different parts of the aquarium (this ensures

A typical thermostatically controlled heater hangs on the rim of the aquarium protruding from the water's surface. Submersible heaters are also available.

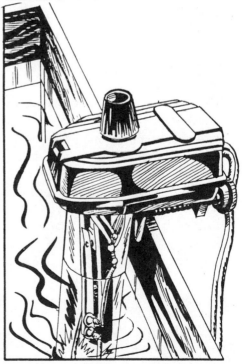

Outfitting the Aquarium

be partly compensated for by fitting the air stone underneath or beside the heating tube. Then the heater is constantly surrounded by new water not yet warmed up, and the thermostat does not switch off until all the water in the tank has reached the desired temperature. If we use a separate heater and thermostat, the two instruments are preferably fitted at two corners that are diagonal to each other.

Be careful that no one adjusts the heater without knowing what they are doing. Turning it too high might cook the fish, while turning it too low can freeze them.

that all the water is evenly heated; with a combined heater and thermostat there is the danger that the instrument switches off before the whole aquarium has reached the desired temperature); finally it could happen that thermostat or heater develop a fault—then, if we have a combined heater and thermostat, we lack both instruments, although one of them would still be able to function.

The disadvantages of the combined heater and thermostat can

Outfitting the Aquarium

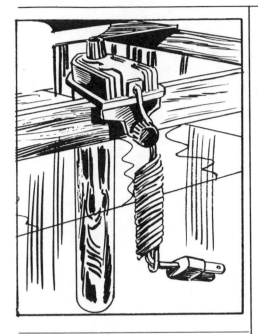

Unfortunately, most aquarium heaters come with short electrical cords. Be sure to use a heavy-duty extension if you can't reach the electrical outlet with the cord provided.

Odds and Ends

Apart from the actual aquarium, lights, heater, and the filter, there are other small pieces of equipment that we will need.

A net is absolutely essential for taking fishes out of the aquarium. Only a rectangular shape is of use. The size should be about 8 × 12 centimeters. Two nets are better

than one, because then we can drive the fishes with one net into the other. Often a glass container has an advantage over the net, because the fishes are frequently easier to catch with the nearly invisible glass receptacle.

The glass panes of our aquarium will very soon be overgrown with algae. This looks ugly and untidy and reduces visibility. We, therefore, require a window cleaner. In the simplest form, this is a razor blade holder with a length of 50 centimeters. The plastic window cleaners frequently offered do not scratch the glass panes as easily as a razor blade does, but on the other hand they do not cope with the algal growth quite so effortlessly.

To change the water we need a siphon tube. We could use a rubber

A siphon is handy to get heavy mulm from the bottom of the tank.

Outfitting the Aquarium

hose but a transparent plastic tube is better, for at some stage the tube is bound to get blocked by small stones, humus, or plant debris washed up with the water. Then it helps to be able to see where the particles are lodged. Since we not only remove water with the tube, but suck off silt as well, a settling chamber would be useful to have. It is connected to the end of the tube and prevents siphoning off sand and gravel as well as the silt.

Equally essential, of course, is a thermometer, which we attach to a side pane of the aquarium or allow to float freely. On no account must

Siphon tubes with self-starting features are available at your local pet shop. Your pet shop will also have a stick-on thermometer (upper figure).

we rely on our skin when we check the water temperature; a simple and cheap thermometer is decidedly more reliable. A food ring for dried food and a sifter for *Tubifex* worms complete our equipment.

The Biological Equilibrium

All natural waters, including lakes, ponds, rivers, and streams, are governed by a biological equilibrium. With the aid of sunlight and inorganic mineral salts, water plants, particularly algae, produce organic substances from carbon dioxide. Some of these plants may be devoured by plant eating animals that in turn are the prey of predatory fishes. The excreta and cadavers of the animals as well as the dead plants are decomposed by

Make sure your siphon is long enough or it might splatter all over the floor.

bacteria and converted back into inorganic substances, including carbon dioxide (called carbonic acid when in solution) and minerals. From carbon dioxide and minerals live green plants, again with the help of sunlight, build up their organic substance. During this process, known as photosynthesis, where inorganic substances produce organic substances, plants give off oxygen. This oxygen is used for respiration by animals and plants; that is, they use it for "burning up" nutrients, which again results in the production of carbon dioxide. We thus get a cycle of these substances that is kept going by plants, bacteria, and animals. If this cycle proceeds without disruption, we talk of the "biological equilibrium."

This kind of biological equilibrium is only possible in larger waters. In the past it used to be thought that a biological equilibrium could be achieved in the aquarium as well. It was assumed that the plants would supply sufficient oxygen for the respiration of the fishes; one actually imagined the waste products of the fishes could be utilized completely by the plants. Experience and calculations have shown that this is not so. Perhaps it would be possible in a 50-gallon tank that is well planted

The Biological Equilibrium

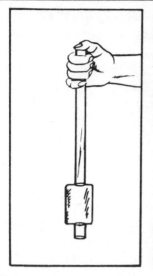
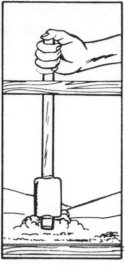
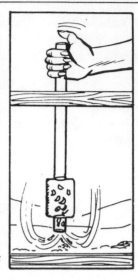

and well illuminated to achieve a biological equilibrium if one put a single guppy in it. But who would install an expensive tank like that and then only keep one fish of barely three centimeters length in it!

It is not, then, much of a biological equilibrium that is "automatically maintained in the aquarium." We have to try to maintain the equilibrium in our tanks by supplying oxygen and removing carbon dioxide, both done by aeration, and we have to remove the waste products of the fishes by regular water changes and filtration or convert them to harmless substances by the biological filter.

Every aquarist needs to know a little bit about aquarium biology and

The dip tube is a handy gadget. You hold your thumb over the top before you put it into the tank, locate the dirt to be removed, then lift your thumb. The water and dirt are sucked into the chamber immediately. Then put your thumb back over the tube and remove it, with the debris, to a garbage can.

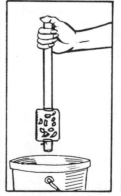
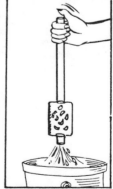

The Biological Equilibrium

aquarium chemistry. I shall try here to describe the problems as simply and comprehensively as possible.

Chemistry

Animals breathe in oxygen and breathe out carbon dioxide. We have already learned this at school. There are many people who incorrectly believe it is exactly the other way around where plants are concerned: that they breathe in carbon dioxide and breathe out oxygen. But this is a misconception. Plants also breathe in oxygen and breathe out carbon dioxide. But over and above that another process goes on, as I have already mentioned: photosynthesis. Photosynthesis is only possible in green plants. During this process they build up organic substances

You must have a working knowledge of aquarium chemistry if you are going to be successful in maintaining and breeding aquarium fishes. It isn't complicated, and even children can understand it.

The Biological Equilibrium

from carbon dioxide and water and give off oxygen. The energy for this process is supplied by the light. That is, photosynthesis can only take place when the plants are illuminated and only then do the plants produce oxygen. During the night the plants do not supply any oxygen; on the contrary, they use up oxygen for respiration.

Aquarium plants produce oxygen in the sunshine; they give off carbon dioxide during darkness. Plants are not capable of producing enough oxygen for fishes to utilize.

Two important terms in aquarium chemistry are pH and hardness. What do we mean by them? The pH informs us about the degree of acidity of water. pH 7 describes a neutral water, pH above seven characterizes alkaline water (the more alkaline, the higher the pH),

pH below seven describes acid water (the more acid, the lower the pH). The pH is measured with indicator solutions, paper, or electronically. The paper method consists of small strips of paper that are dipped into the water and, depending on the pH, assume a certain shade of color. This shade of color is compared with a chart (supplied along with the paper). A pH above eight may be considered harmful, and at pH nine many freshwater fishes are already unable to live. In the same way, a pH below 5.5 to 6 is already too acid for many fishes.

Every housewife knows what "hard water" implies. In hard water soap does not lather; for washing, hard water uses up more soap than does "soft water"; hard water also causes ugly whitish spots on drinking glasses that are merely drained but not wiped dry. The hardness of the water depends above all on the amount of calcium dissolved in the water. Hardness is recorded in degrees of German hardness (DH). The more degrees of hardness a water is found to have, the harder it is. Soft water has degrees of hardness of 0 to 8. Extremely hard water may reach a hardness of 30 or more. There are relatively simple methods by which you can measure the hardness of

48

The Biological Equilibrium

water. If you wish to know how hard your tap water is, the simplest way is to just phone your local waterworks and they will give you prompt and reliable information.

There is a certain connection between pH and hardness. Calcium bicarbonate, which is mainly responsible for water hardness, makes the water slightly alkaline at the same time.

Many tropical fishes thrive best in slightly acid, soft water, but some require very hard, very alkaline water. If one wants to breed fishes, there are many species where one has to make sure the quality of the water is suitable. In most cases the water in the breeding aquarium must be neither alkaline nor too hard.

So now we know why aquarists hate calcium so much. Without chemical aids, there is nothing much we can do about the calcium automatically supplied to us with the tap water. But we can at least see to it that we do not put additional calcium into the water by, for instance, decorating it with limestone or using a calcareous material for the bottom layer.

Most tropical fishes thrive in water that is slightly acid. That's the problem with a community tank. . .what pH. . .how much hardness. . .what to feed and when.

The Biological Equilibrium

Biogenic Decalcification

In the past it used to be thought that the plants in an aquarium were able to change hard water into soft water. One spoke about "biogenic decalcification," a decalcification due to living organisms. Today we know that in the aquarium biogenic decalcification occurs no more often than the ominous biological equilibrium. This does not mean, however, that biogenic decalcification does not exist. It has an important part to play in nature. Large and deep lakes, for instance, almost always contain much softer water than do the tributaries that supply them with water. By biogenic decalcification, a large percentage of the calcium supplied to these lakes is precipitated. But, in the aquarium it is a different matter altogether: the very small quantities of calcium that with luck are precipitated during the day are dissolved again by the water during the night. How does this happen?

If we bring hard water to a boil in a saucepan, calcium deposits will form at the sides of the pan. All housewives know and fear this "scale." Calcium is water soluble in the form of calcium bicarbonate, but as calcium carbonate it scarcely dissolves. When we heat water, the carbon dioxide dissolved in the water is driven out of solution, and part of the calcium bicarbonate is precipitated as calcium carbonate. A similar process takes place in the illuminated aquarium. If they receive sufficient light, plants use up the carbon dioxide in the water. If only a little dissolved carbon dioxide is present, the plants remove part of the carbon dioxide they need from calcium bicarbonate. What remains is calcium carbonate, which is precipitated in the form of a calcium crust. When we observe aquatic plants in nature, we will often find that their leaves are covered with a fairly thick, crumbling crust of calcium carbonate. In the aquarium this phenomenon is less frequent, but it does occur from time to time, for instance on the leaves of *Echinodorus maior*.

Thus the water is made softer by the photosynthesis of the plants. But that does not help us much, because by night animals and plants discharge carbon dioxide that is taken up by the calcium carbonate; this once again becomes calcium bicarbonate and dissolves in the water. We speak of this process as biogenic calcification. There would only be a surplus of undissolved calcium—that is, true decalcification—if the plants were able to take in more carbonic acid than they and the animals give off again during respiration. But such ideal conditions will not be found in any aquarium, for the waste products of the fishes and the uneaten foods are constantly being broken down by bacteria, again producing carbon dioxide. Since we almost always have a certain excess of carbon dioxide in the aquarium, it will usually be the biogenic calcification that is predominant.

Nitrogen Compounds

The theories of biological equilibrium and biogenic decalcification have not caused much damage in aquaristics. These theories used to play an important part in the discussions of the aquarists, but not so in their practice. The so-called "old water theory," however, is a different story altogether. For many years it was believed that the older aquarium water was, the better it was, and there were aquarists who were proud of having water in their aquarium that was five years old or even older. Whether such liquid manure deserves to be called "water" at all seems doubtful.

Fish feed, digest, and eliminate. Urine and feces are produced. These excreta are converted into soluble substances by bacteria, they are broken down and mineralized, i.e., changed back into inorganic substances. During this process many soluble nitrogen compounds develop (ammonia, nitrite, nitrate), only a small percentage of which is taken up again by the plants. If they accumulate excessively, these nitrogen compounds are harmful for the fishes and plants. They inhibit growth and reproductive ability, and they make animals and plants susceptible to pathogenic organisms.

To keep the poisonous nitrogenous substances in check, we must: (1) carry out partial water changes at regular intervals (either daily, biweekly, weekly, or whatever is needed for the health of the particular aquarium involved). To do this siphon off about 25% to 50% of the old water and replace it with fresh water (preferably aged 24 hours) of the same temperature and chemistry. The smaller our tank is and the more fishes we are keeping in it, the more frequently we have to change the water and the more water we have to replace. (2) Maintain proper filtration. The filters must be kept operating efficiently at all times and the filter

Water Types

material must be cleaned periodically. And (3) a biological filter must be in operation. A biological filter consists of the bacteria that transform the poisonous nitrogenous compounds to less harmful nitrates that can be utilized by the plants. The bacteria develop in the filter where they constantly have material to feed on (in the case of the undergravel filter they exist in the gravel itself), usually in the form of ammonia compounds that they convert to nitrites. The nitrites are also poisonous but they are converted by other bacteria to nitrates. Nitrates are removed by the plants and by the periodic water changes. Test kits are available to follow the biological action so that fishes are not placed in an aquarium that has a lethal concentration of nitrites or ammonia. All newly setup tanks go through this nitrogen cycle but usually settle down to a safe level after about two weeks.

What is Water?

Chemically, as you will probably remember from school, water is H_2O. That is, it is a compound of two atoms of hydrogen and one atom of oxygen. However, in aquaria pure water is not much use to us, since the water we require is an aqueous solution of various substances. Water is a good solvent, so we find mineral salts, gases, and organic substances in natural or tap water. Depending on the salinity, we differentiate between fresh water, brackish water, and sea water. Most natural inland waters—and, of course, our tap water as well—are fresh water. The salinity of fresh water is so slight that we cannot taste it. If the salt content rises so much that our tongue is able to perceive it—as, for instance, in the deltas of rivers or in sea areas with a low salt content—we speak of brackish water, which has a salt content of between 0.5 and 2%. The salinity of sea water lies between 2 and 4%.

Your aquarium water may well come from your tap. Contact your local water company and ask them for the chemical components and characteristics of your tap water.

Water Types

Fresh Water

From our taps we get a water that—however much it may vary from one town to another—we can use for almost all freshwater fishes. In fact, the so much despised tap water actually has a great advantage for us: since it is meant for human consumption, it is carefully examined for harmful substances by the water companies. Thus we can say that drinking water that does not harm babies and small children is safe for most freshwater fishes, too. There are, of course, exceptions. Fishes coming from waters with a particularly low salt content require, at least for their cultivation, water that is very soft and generally slightly acid. Conversely, there are fishes that live in fresh waters with a particularly high salinity, and here we even have to add salt to their water. We use non-iodized table salt for this purpose or, better yet, synthetic sea salts.

We must not, however, in order to simplify matters, say that this water has a high and that water a low salinity. We should speak of hard and soft water, since the salinity of fresh water depends mainly on the minerals that are responsible for the hardness of the water. As already mentioned, water of 0 to 4 DH is considered to be very soft, up to 8 DH to be soft, above 12 DH to be hard, and above 18 DH to be very hard.

To soften a water that is too hard, we can dilute it with distilled water or rain water. But with rain water we have to be careful. If collected from dusty, dirty roofs, especially in the city, it might contain highly poisonous substances. Only the water running off after a long period of rain can be used, for here it can be assumed that most of the dangerous substances have been rinsed away. The application of distilled water is too expensive as a rule. Softening with ion exchangers, the best method, requires a basic knowledge of chemistry.

For the great majority of freshwater fishes we can without hesitation use the water coming from our taps. Even if chlorine has been added to it, we need not worry. Within a split second the free chlorine will combine with organic substances dissolved in the water. Water containing chlorine could only become dangerous for fishes if the latter were put straight into water which has just come from the tap. In a furnished aquarium the bottom layer and water contain such a lot of organic substances that the chlorine that slipped in during the changing of the water is used up instantly and is changed into perfectly harmless chlorides. If you still feel uneasy about this, you can let the water stand in a bucket for a few hours or overnight with an airstone. Then the chlorine escapes.

Brackish Water

Brackish water, a mixture of sea water and fresh water, is of advantage for the keeping of certain fishes. These are mainly all fish species originating from mixed-water

Marine tanks can use coral skeletons. . .so can brackish water tanks. . .but freshwater tanks might dissolve the coral.

zones near the coast. Many of them can be kept for a long period both in pure sea water and in pure fresh water. Prepare brackish water by mixing fresh water and sea water, varying the concentration as desired (the concentration of brackish water and sea water is determined with a hydrometer purchasable at aquarium shops). With brackish water, a seawater addition of a mere 10% often improves the well-being of the fish. Fishes from brackish waters are generally slightly more delicate than other fishes; we shall not, therefore, recommend them to the beginner.

Sea Water

Great progress has been made in seawater aquaristics, the care of sea animals in the aquarium, over the last few years. And yet the care of sea fishes is considerably more difficult than that of freshwater fishes; the novice should start off with a freshwater aquarium. On the other hand, there are, however, many lower animals that even a beginner can keep in the seawater tank: crabs, starfishes, certain anemones. If you want to begin with the care of seawater animals, you should first of all keep animals from the Mediterranean or North

Water Types

American coast, because they are not as sensitive to temperature changes as are animals from either tropical or cold seas.

If we require sea water, it is by no means necessary to order it in water cans or barrels from the coast. We can mix it ourselves by dissolving synthetic sea salts (available at pet shops) in tap or distilled water as directed.

Cold or Warm?

Native fishes do not normally need a heated tank. That is why many beginners believe cold water fishes were easier to keep than tropical warm water fishes. This is only a half-truth. In winter we need not worry if we keep cold water fishes, since it will not harm them if the temperature happens to drop to 10 °C or even lower. But in summer the cold water fishes might present a problem. If the water temperature becomes too high, they are not comfortable because warm water cannot dissolve as much oxygen as cold water. Stream fishes, for instance, particularly fishes from mountain brooks, are generally adapted to water with a high oxygen content; they easily die of asphyxia in summer when the water gets too

warm or when dirt leads to additional oxygen depletion. To heat an aquarium with warm water fishes is no problem at all. But there is no inexpensive device that could be used to cool a cold water aquarium on hot summer days.

The assumption that tropical fishes are more beautiful than native fishes is completely erroneous. Many of our native fishes (for instance, the darters) are hardly less richly colored than tropical fishes, and the aquarist who observes his fishes well will detect—even in cold water fishes—interesting modes of behavior, fine shapes, and beautiful colors.

The so-called "local aquarium," however, with native fishes and native plants, usually remains a dream that cannot be fulfilled. Many native water plants lose their leaves and lie dormant in winter. Even if we can offer them great quantities of light in the summer, a "true" local aquarium will stand empty and barren in winter. With a bit of cheating we can improve matters quite easily. Plant the cold water tank with tropical or subtropical aquatic plants that are able to tolerate low temperatures. If you can put up your aquarium in front of a window facing north or east, you will get enough daylight to

Plants

be able to keep very light-hungry eel grass *(Vallisneria)* and water weed *(Elodea)*. If, in addition, you plant a few milfoil shoots *(Myriophyllum)*, then the native fishes, too, can hide themselves in this abundant plant growth.

One may regret it, but it remains a fact that the cold water aquarium is going out of existence. Increasingly more aquarists keep only tropical fishes and, consequently, the pet shops only rarely offer even a few cold water fishes nowadays.

The biological actions and requirements of plants have already been referred to in various parts of this book. Light is essential for good plant growth, but some plant species need a great deal of light, and others need less. There are even plants that die if they are illuminated too strongly. By and large, however, we can say that, with the illumination commonly used, our aquarium plants get too little light rather than too much.

Many people keep an aquarium because they love aquascaping, with bright green plants contrasting with lovely colored fishes.

Captions for Color Plates
A Three-spot or Blue Gourami, *Trichogaster trichopterus.* Photo by H.J. Richter, p. 57. A Red Siamese Fighting Fish, *Betta splendens.* Photo by H.J. Richter, p. 58. A Zebra Angelfish, *Pterophyllum scalare,* p. 59. Marbled Angelfish, *Pterophyllum scalare.* Photo by H.J. Richter, pp. 60-61. Neon Tetras, *Paracheirodon innesi.* Photo by Dr. Herbert R. Axelrod, p. 62. Three-lined Pencilfish, *Nannostomus marginatus.* Photo by H.J. Richter, p. 63. Mixed high-fin Swordtails and Platies. Photo by Dr. Karl Knaack, p. 64.

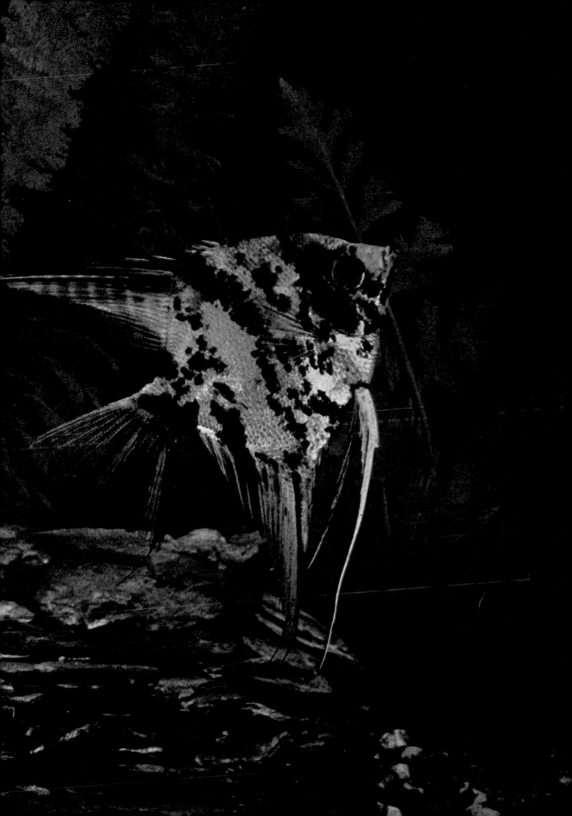

Plants

Light Requirements

A rule of thumb for the light requirements of individual species is difficult to draw up. As already mentioned, it all very much depends on where the aquarium is located. The best, if not the quickest and cheapest, method is to proceed by trial and error. Plants that thrive well in our aquarium are cultivated by, for instance, letting their shoots grow into new plants or by purchasing further specimens. Conversely, plants that will not thrive in spite of good care are removed.

On the average, one can say that an aquarium that is 50 to 60 centimeters long and 25 to 30 cm deep requires a fluorescent tube of 20 watts. If the tank is twice as deep, we have to supply it with at least double, but preferably three times, the amount of light. If we use incandescent lamps, these figures should be trebled, i.e. instead of 20 watts (fluorescent lamp) we use 60 watts (incandescent lamps).

Arrangement

How do we arrange the plants in the aquarium? After all, they are not there just to utilize and remove waste materials and to supply oxygen; first and foremost they are meant to decorate the tank. The foreground of the aquarium is planted with species that remain small; those in the background should be large and tall. Medium-sized plants are arranged in the center. Plants with modest light requirements, like the cryptocorynes, are arranged in such a way that they are shaded to some extent by tall and broad-leaved plants. Very large plants are put in singly to ensure they can spread themselves out sufficiently without hindering other plants. Smaller plants, on the other hand, are put into one hole in groups. Plants of the same species should be standing together in the aquarium. They should form colonies.

Finally, we should also think of the fishes when we arrange our plants. Many fishes appreciate it when they find hiding places in the plant thicket. An equal number of fishes require a large open swimming space.

Therefore, furnish one part of the aquarium with a dense growth of bushy plants and in another part leave sufficient swimming space. It is also advisable not to put in too many plants to start off with. Once the plants have taken root and begun to spread out, the "jungle" will soon have to be thinned out anyway.

How do we put in the plants? First the bottom material is put into the aquarium, then the "dead" decorations, and, finally, the tank is half filled with water. After that, start to plant the foreground. That is, begin with the smallest plants and work through to the back. If you have experience with the planting of a garden, this knowledge will be of use to you here. First draw a proper planting plan, a sketch that shows how you intend to distribute the plants. The plants are put into the sand upright; this goes above all for the roots, which should not be bent upward. The rootstock should go far enough into the ground so that the "heart" of the plant—the part where the leaves develop—remains free. If the plant sits too deep, it will not grow properly or will even die. Plants that already possess roots are trimmed slightly at the bottom to promote the new root formation. The multiplication of stalk-forming plants can be encouraged by dividing the stalk in much the same way as housewives do with *Tradescantia*, the well-known hanging plant. Many aquarium plants put forth shoots.

The freshly planted aquarium is first of all left in peace for 10 days so that the plants can recuperate and grow roots. Only then are the animals put in. If everything grows well, we have to thin out the plant stock from time to time. To do this, cut off the uppermost shoots of stalk-forming plants, in this way achieving bushy growth. From other plants remove the outside (older) leaves, or take out whole plants. Some species grow so rapidly and strongly that we have to keep removing the newly formed young plants. For this, first separate the young shoots from the runner connecting them with the mother plant and carefully pull them out of the bottom layer, roots and all.

Suitable Plants

The following list of plants had to be restricted to a very small selection of recommendable aquarium plants.

Cold Water Plants

Hornwort *(Ceratophyllum)* Can be planted anywhere in the tank or used as a floating plant

Anacharis *(Elodea)* See hornwort; several stalks are planted together

Plants

Duckweed *(Lemna)* Exclusively as a floating plant on the water surface

Ludwigia Particularly suitable for the planting of the front corners

Milfoil *(Myriophyllum)* See *Ludwigia*

In addition our cold water tank can also be planted with various less delicate aquatic plants from other parts of the world. Particularly suitable are Arrowworts *(Sagittaria)* and Eel grass *(Vallisneria)* Pronouncedly exotic plants do not thrive in the unheated aquarium.

Warm Water Plants

Sword plants *(Aponogeton)* Medium to high growing plants that should not be directly in the foreground but not in the background either

Fanworts *(Cabomba)* In clusters between dark green plants for contrast. Requires plenty of light and, therefore, best planted under the light. Grows well in cold water aquaria

Water sprite *(Ceratopteris thalicroides)* Suitable for planting along the edges

Cryptocorynes *(Cryptocoryne)* Abundantly growing, polymorphic group of plants. Some are short, some tall, and must be arranged accordingly. Several species are relatively undemanding and suitable for beginners.

Small-leaved Amazon sword plant *(Echinodorus brevipedicellatus)* As a central, eye-catching plant, it must not be wedged in between other plants. Very decorative

Cellophane sword plant *(E. cordifolius)* As above with very broad heart-shaped leaves

Dwarf Amazon sword plant *(E. latifolius)* Foreground plant; forms a "lawn"

Indian water star *(Hygrophila polysperma)* Use several shoots for planting the edges of the bottom layer

Ambulia *(Limnophila)* *Limnophila indica* is poisonous. Take care!

Temple plant *(Nomaphila stricta)* As for water star but with considerably larger leaves

Crystalwort *(Riccia fluitans)* Floating plant forming mats

Arrowworts *(Sagittaria)* The dwarf arrowwort in particular is a lawn-forming foreground plant

Water wisteria *(Synemma triflorum)* See water star; with large, fissured leaves

Eel grasses *(Vallisneria)* The eel grasses are particularly

Fishes

suitable for planting the background and sides.

Java moss. Rearing plant for wood and stones, can also be put into the aquarium in tussock form.

It is because of the fishes that we are taking all the trouble and we should really devote a much longer chapter to them than we are able to do here. We have to confine ourselves to the most important matters. If you wish to know more you will find much information in other books published by TFH.

First we must determine which fishes can be put into one and the same tank. Cold and warm water fishes do not belong together nor do predatory and peaceable fishes. We have to remember that most of the so-called peaceable fishes also turn into predators if we put them into a tank with much smaller species or with smaller members of their own species. The little ones are then not regarded as fellow lodgers but as better water fleas meant to be eaten. Many fishes that do not practice proper brood care devour their eggs and their offspring if they are able to get near them. This is why we use special aquaria for the breeding of fishes, so that eggs or fry and

parent animals can be quickly separated. The cultivation of fishes is the most beautiful experience for the aquarist. Only during spawning do the animals develop their full activity and attractiveness; over and above that the mere fact that they are spawning tells us they are being well and correctly cared for. Fishes that are not very well looked after do not usually reproduce in the aquarium.

Livebearers

Some fish species breed "automatically." We do not need to contribute anything. This applies, for instance, to most livebearers which are quite impossible to prevent from continuously giving forth young (which, in the mixed tank, then constitute a welcome delicacy not only for the other fishes but also for their own parents). Livebearers, as opposed to most egg-laying fishes, practice internal fertilization. Not until four weeks after fertilization, after the belly of the female has grown increasingly bigger, are the young born. In some species, the posterior abdominal region grows darker during pregnancy (pregnancy spot). Provided we want our fishes to have

Fishes

any offspring at all the pregnant females are best put into a well-planted breeding tank (all-glass or plastic tank of 40 × 25 × 25 centimeters).Once the young animals are born the females are taken out of the container.

Egg Layers

With regard to egg-laying fishes, the male does not usually fertilize the eggs until the female has discharged them. To breed egg-laying fishes, we therefore have to put the couples into the breeding container. For fishes up to a length of about 6 centimeters, a breeding aquarium of the above mentioned size is sufficient. Fish eggs are often sensitive to bacteria and microscopically small animalcules, hence the aquarium should be thoroughly cleaned. This goes for furnishings and plants as well as for container, bottom material, and stones. It may be suitable to treat the aquarium, without fishes of course, with a dark red solution of potassium permanganate or a suitable commercial preparation for about ten minutes. Afterward everything is very thoroughly rinsed with running tap water. Some plants do not survive this drastic treatment, but then the harmful micro-organisms are destroyed, too, or at least decimated.

For free spawners and plant spawners a bush of fine foliaged plants should be provided—perhaps a good handful of Java moss. For bottom spawners a layer of thoroughly boiled peat fibers is useful. Bubblenest spawners appreciate a cover of floating plants (such as crystalwort, *Riccia*, or water sprite). For substrate and cave spawners, put a small flower pot or a cleaned coconut shell into the tank.

Mild aeration is favorable in the breeding aquarium, too. A glass cover is essential, because spawning fishes usually swim vigorously and frequently leap out of the water.

If the parent animals do not exercise brood care (this depends on the species) take them out of the breeding container after spawning. Almost all free and plant spawners leave their brood to its fate after spawning (or even regard them as delicious caviar). We could, of course, even remove the parents of brooding species from the breeding tank, but it is more exciting to leave them with their progeny. The devoted brood-care of some fishes is a special experience for everyone, even the most experienced aquarist.

Beginner's Fishes

Brood care is exercised above all by cichlids and the bubblenest building labyrinthfishes. The cichlids often still protect their young in the shoal for a long period. But where the labyrinthfishes are concerned the brooding impulse dies as soon as the young leave the nest and start to swim independently. Also it is only the male labyrinthfish as a rule who looks after the brood; therefore always remove the female after spawning. When the fry are swimming independently the father is fished out, too, for however devotedly he may have been looking after the eggs, now he might be a danger to the free-swimming fish.

Just one more word on the question most frequently puzzling us: how can we tell males and females apart? With some species we know by the difference in color: the colors of the males are usually stronger and more beautiful. Hints may also be supplied by the shape and size of the fins and here again the males have usually been favored by nature. But with a great many fishes we cannot detect any difference in shape or color between the sexes. Here we have to "guess" who is who by watching their behavior and by the slightly swollen belly of the female.

Here we will deal briefly with a few of the common typical fishes that a beginner is likely to buy and try to keep. Most of the following fishes are readily available, are cheap, and are easy to keep in home aquaria if well cared for. Some are not difficult to breed, and some, like the livebearers, are hard to *keep* from reproducing. We will consider first the characters of the main families and then a few common species of each.

Carp-like Fishes, Family Cyprinidae

This gigantic family of mostly small fishes contributes many species to the aquarium hobby. Many beautiful species are found in North America, and also some in Europe, but these are generally cold water fishes that are not kept in aquaria. Our popular species come mostly from Asia, and a few species are from Africa. To this family belong the barbs, danios, rasboras, and goldfish. All have only one fin on the back (dorsal fin), and never have an adipose fin between the dorsal and tail (caudal) fins. Many species have barbels at the corners of the mouth. Body shape varies from slender, elongate species to deep-bodied, robust forms. Some are active swimmers, while a few are shyer and less active. Most species are schooling fishes and should be kept in small groups, never singly. All species lay eggs, and most will eat their eggs and young if given the chance. Most will take flake foods, but prefer live food and plant matter.

The danios, genera *Danio* and *Brachydanio*, are attractive, active, schooling fishes found from India to Borneo. They should be kept in groups, not just one or two fish, in tanks providing a lot of plant cover as well as much free swimming space. Being hardy fishes, they are not hard to please as long as the temperature remains warm, the water clean, and they are well fed—dry food is accepted.

Males are distinguished from females by their brighter colors and more active behavior. Females ready to spawn usually have the abdomen swollen with eggs and are duller than the males. Isolate breeding pairs in small tanks containing thick clumps of fine-leaved plants and place the tank in a well lighted area. Danios are prolific spawners, but also are prolific spawn eaters—remove the parents as soon as spawning is completed. The young hatch in a day and begin to feed on very fine food in a few days.

The zebra danio, *Brachydanio rerio*, pearl danio, *Brachydanio albolineatus*, and giant danio, *Danio aequipinnatus*, are the species most commonly seen. All are attractive, peaceful fishes.

Barbs of the genera *Barbus*, *Barbodes*, *Capoeta*, or *Puntius*, are stockier-bodied than danios and are more vigorous. There is a strong tendency toward nipping fins and bothering smaller fishes, so keep a careful eye on them if in a community tank. Barbs spend most of their time chasing each other around the bottom of the tank, so don't mistake this for a courtship dance. Males are slimmer and more colorful than females. Spawning occurs much as in danios. *Capoeta tetrazona*, the tiger barb, is the most commonly seen species.

Rasboras, especially the commonly kept *Rasbora heteromorpha*, are small, peaceful fish that should be kept in relatively large schools. They are easy to keep as long as the water is kept warm and not too hard. All types of food are taken. Males are slenderer than females and, in *Rasbora heteromorpha*, have a fine gold line above the black triangle. Breeding is not especially difficult if the water is soft. The eggs are adhesive and are attached

Beginner's Fishes

either on the underside of a large leaf or to the stems of other plants.

The American Tetras, Family Characidae, and Their Relatives

The tetras or characins are closely related to the Cyprinidae and might be considered the South American version of the cyprinids. A few families occur in Africa, but most are found in Central and South America. There are many species in this group, and large numbers, both of species and individuals, are kept in aquaria. Although many species resemble barbs or rasboras in shape, all lack barbels on the jaws and many have an adipose fin (fleshy, without rays or supports) between the dorsal and caudal fins. The keeping and breeding of many species is very difficult, and specialized literature should be seen if you intend keeping uncommon species of tetras. A few of the most common aquarium species are listed below. Most require soft water and fine-foliaged plants for breeding. Many are schooling fishes and almost all carnivorous. The most spectacular fishes belonging to this group are probably the piranhas, but these large fishes are not

suitable for beginning aquarists.

Black tetras, *Gymnocorymbus ternetzi* and *G. thayeri*, are attractive deep-bodied fishes with large dorsal and anal fins. The color is often very dark, almost black, with two broad vertical bars on the anterior half of the fish. Breeding is relatively simple.

Pristella, often called the X-ray fish, is a small, beautiful tetra from northern South America. The color pattern, especially the red tail fin, is very attractive, and the fish are peaceful and easy to keep. An albino variety is commonly sold and considered by many people to be very attractive.

Many tetras belonging to the genera *Hemigrammus* and *Hyphessobrycon* are colorful and easily kept in the aquarium. Species of *Hemigrammus* include the glowlight tetra, *H. erythrozonus*, the head and tail light, *H. ocellifer*, and the rummy-nose tetra, *H. rhodostomus*. *Hyphessobrycon* contains such beautiful species as the rosy tetra, *H. bentosi rosaceus*, flame tetra, *H. flammeus*, and flag tetra, *H. heterorhabdus*. *Paracheirodon* is best known for the colorful neon tetra, *P. innesi*, and the cardinal tetra, *P. axelrodi*. The neon is known to every aquarist, although it was only discovered in the 1930s. It is often confused by

72

Beginner's Fishes

beginners with the equally beautiful cardinal tetra which has a similar pattern of blue and red. The cardinal is more slender than the neon, and its brighter red color extends from the snout to the tail, while that of the neon is only on the posterior half of the body.

The pencilfishes, genus *Nannostomus,* are often seen and are closely related to the tetras. They are put in the family Lebiasinidae. The slim body, pointed head, and distinctive striped colors make them beautiful aquarium fishes. All are peaceful, but they should be kept in small groups or schools. Because of their small size, some species should not be kept in community tanks containing larger fish.

Gasteropelecidae is the name given to the family containing the unusual hatchetfishes. They are easily recognized by their highly compressed shape, very deep chest, and the high placement of the pectoral fins. The few species are all very similar.

Armored Catfishes, Family Callichthyidae

Although there are a great number of different catfishes belonging to many families on the market, the beginner is most likely to pick up a small bronze or peppered corydoras *Corydoras aeneus* and *C. paleatus,* or one of the many other species available, as a scavenger for his tank. *Corydoras* are easily maintained, peaceful catfishes that do a good job cleaning up some of the debris and leftovers of the other tank inhabitants. Don't expect them to live only on scraps, however; they should be fed like their tankmates.

Livebearers, Family Poeciliidae

This family of common aquarium livebearers is restricted to the Americas, most species being found in Central America and the northern part of South America. In these fishes the anal fin of the male is changed into a structure called the gonopodium, used to introduce sperm into the female's body. Sexes are thus easily distinguished in all the species. The eggs develop within the mother's body and, after a month to month and a half, the fry are born. As a rule, the livebearers are easy to keep and breed, in fact so easy that one can end up with too many fish if not careful. The main problems come from the small size of the young,

Beginner's Fishes

which are choice food for many other fishes, including their parents. Thus a pregnant female should be isolated in a plastic or mesh breeding chamber where the young fall through slits in a false bottom into a safe compartment below. If no such cage is available, a heavily planted aquarium should give some of the young protection from other fishes.

Although many livebearers have been kept in aquaria, only four types, guppies, mollies, swordtails, and platies, are commonly kept by beginners. The guppy and molly belong to the genus *Poecilia* (formerly the guppy was put in the genus *Lebistes* and the molly in *Mollienesia)*, while the swords and platies belong to the genus *Xiphophorus.*

Guppies, *Poecilia reticulata,* are known to every aquarist. Almost every store that sells tropical fishes sells some type originally found in northern South America. These small fish are attractive and easy to keep. Males are at least spotted with red and blue, while the much larger females are plain gray. There are a great number of aquarium varieties showing an incredible range of color and fin shape. Some domestic strains have males that are larger than females of the wild type. There are many books on raising

guppies and societies of guppy enthusiasts.

Poecilia sphenops is the molly most suitable to the beginner's tank. It is not as attractive as the species with very large dorsal fins, but one has a better chance of keeping and breeding this fish than the fancier species. All mollies require hard water, and a small amount of added salt will do no harm. Feed mollies live foods whenever available, but mollies will also take dry foods; all require a large amount of vegetable matter in the diet.

The common swordtail, *Xiphophorus helleri,* is a popular aquarium fish with beginners and experts alike. Originally imported from Mexico, the modern swordtail is available in a broad variety of color patterns, ranging from the original greenish with red stripes, solid reds, red and blacks, to high fin types and albinos. Males have the lower part of the caudal fin enlarged into a long "sword." The genetics of swordtails is fairly well known, and many people breed them for particular colors or fin shapes. Other species of swordtails are known but are not too commonly imported.

Platies, *Xiphophorus maculatus* and *X. variatus,* are other very popular aquarium fishes renowned for their many different color strains. The species hybridize easily with each other and with the swordtail. Common varieties are wagtails, gold, sunset, blue, and tuxedo platies. Platies are easy to keep and breed, and their bright colors add life to any aquarium.

Cichlids, Family Cichlidae

This large family of bass-like fishes occurs mainly in Central and South America and in Africa. There are many genera and species and many of them have been kept in aquaria at one time or another. Most species are too expensive, large, and difficult to be of much interest to the novice. Many common species are aggressive toward other fishes and require a large tank. Only a few of the more popular and easily kept species are mentioned. The discus, *Symphysodon,* is often a tempting target for the novice, as they are such attractive fish; it is very difficult to keep, however, and the novice would be better off spending his money on something else.

The dwarf cichlids are small American fishes that are often easily kept and bred even in small aquaria. There are many species belonging to the genus *Apistogramma,* but many of these are expensive and little known. The golden dwarf, *Nannacara anomola,* is easily bred even in a 5-gallon tank. The flowing fins of the male, red-edged when ready for breeding, are especially attractive. Females have smaller fins and are swollen with eggs. To get them into best health and color, try feeding exclusively live food for a week or so before trying to spawn them; *Tubifex* worms are greedily accepted. Golden dwarfs spawn on rocks, glass, or, preferably, in a container such as a flower pot turned on its side. Both sexes share the duties of guarding and caring for the eggs, and later for the young.

The kribensis, *Pelvicachromis pulcher* (formerly known as *Pelmatochromis kribensis)* is another small, easily bred species that is popular in aquaria. This species, however, hails from western Africa. Color varieties are commonly sold. The kribensis breeds in much the same fashion as does the golden dwarf.

Although it does not look much like other cichlids, the angelfish, *Pterophyllum scalare,* is also a member of the Cichlidae. It is found in the Amazon basin of South America. Wild fish are silvery with black vertical bars, but there are

Beginner's Fishes

now numerous color varieties available to the hobbyist. These vary from marbled, all-blacks, golden, and blushing angels to forms with normal coloration and greatly enlarged fins, the veil angels. Breeding is relatively easy, especially if you let a group of small fishes mature together and choose their own mates; otherwise the sexes are difficult to distinguish. The eggs are stuck to the glass or a piece of slate placed vertically in the tank. Since the parents may eat the eggs or fry, remove them after spawning.

There are also a large number of other beautiful cichlids on the market that the novice might try his hand at. Many of these are not actually hard to spawn, but it must be remembered that cichlids have large mouths and bad dispositions. They also seem to enjoy uprooting plants and stones from the aquarium bottom. Give them separate tanks with plenty of room and you probably won't have any trouble. Cichlids are among the few fishes that seem to actually become pets in the commonly accepted sense of the word. Some even learn to recognize their owner. Oscars *(Astronotus ocellatus)* and some other large cichlids even seem to enjoy being petted and stroked. African Lake cichlids are easy to breed but require special conditions (hard, alkaline water) and may not be suitable for a beginner.

The Labyrinthfishes

This group includes the popular and well-known bubblenest builders, such as the fighting fish, paradise fish, and the gouramis. All are characterized, in addition to their unusual breeding habits, by having a special organ, the labyrinth, behind the gills. This organ lets the fish use atmospheric air allowing it to survive in water with little dissolved oxygen. When rearing young, the most critical time is the transition from all gill respiration to labyrinth respiration.

Everyone knows the long-finned, graceful betta, the Siamese fighting fish *(Betta splendens)*. The beautiful colors bred into this fish through years of careful breeding are most obvious in the male; females are comparatively drab. While females are often kept in mixed tanks, males are usually put in small bowls or special betta tanks, where they are not able to get at each other and tear fins; the fins are spread fully mainly when another male is in sight.

Paradise fish, *Macropodus*

opercularis, are among the easiest of all fishes to breed. It is unfortunate that they are so nasty in the aquarium; males tend to fight other males and females, while either sex will nip at or kill most fishes of anywhere near the same size. Paradise fish also require lower water temperatures than most tropical fishes, so they should definitely have a tank of their own. This was the first tropical fish to be imported into Europe.

Although several species of small gouramis are easily and cheaply available, few are as popular as the blue gourami, *Trichogaster trichopterus.* This pretty fish and its many color varieties breed in the typical anabantoid fashion. The male blows a large bubblenest, mates with the female, and then places the eggs into the nest. The very small fry stay in the nest for several days and are guarded by the male. After the fry are free-swimming, the male should be removed.

The fishes mentioned on the preceding pages are a mere sampling of the interesting and varied assortment of species available to the beginning hobbyist. The main point to remember when purchasing fishes is to get only those species that fit into your immediate plans.

If you want only pretty fishes and do not care about breeding them, then you have many more possibilities than the breeder. Never overcrowd your fishes or put aggressive species in tanks with other fishes. A good book will give you much of the information necessary for successfully identifying, feeding, housing, and breeding your fishes.

A Varied Diet

Our aquarium fishes are mainly meat-eaters, so what they need most of all is animal protein. But it alone is not sufficient; correct nutrition must also include carbohydrates, fats, and trace substances. More fish species require not only animal food but also plant nourishment than used to be thought.

Dry Food

The pet shops offer a great variety of dried food mixtures. In the past, experienced aquarists regarded dried food as a substitute that a good aquarist gave but unwillingly and only in extreme emergencies. Today this dislike of artificial food is no longer justified to that extent. There are manufacturers who prepare dried flake food according to strictly scientific aspects and test every mixture. So, if our fishes accept dried food at all, we need not hesitate to offer it to them from time to time.

Better, however —and all aquarists agree on this—is live food such as *Tubifex* worms, brine shrimp, midge and mosquito larvae, and insects. A true aquarist goes out in his spare time with fine meshed net and bucket and catches his own food in the nearest pond. It is easier, of course, to buy live food at the pet shop, and if there is no pond anywhere near your home you have no choice but to visit the pet shop once a week.

Tubifex Worms

Tubifex worms are available at almost every pet shop. Another possibility is to take big lumps of these worms out of the mud of nutritious waters, but that is a bit risky. The cleaned *Tubifex* worms that you have either rinsed yourself or bought washed at the pet shop are best put into a covered dish with very little water and kept in the refrigerator. Stored cool, they keep

for quite some time, especially if rinsed once a day. An even better method is to keep the worms in a shallow dish under dripping water.

Infusoria

Some types of live food can be cultured in the home. The microscopically small food animals (infusoria) that are required for the fry shortly after hatching have to be bred at home. If you want to cultivate fishes you also need to give some thought to the food the hatching brood will require. For this purpose it is best to start a culture of slipper animalcules early. A handful of hay and a bit of banana skin are covered with one or two quarts of water, inoculated with aquarium or pond water (or, better still, with a few milliliters from another culture), and then plenty of slipper animalcules can be harvested after one to three weeks. Once we have such a culture of slipper animalcules, it is easy to maintain it. Every few weeks we prepare a new infusion of hay, straw, or finely chopped turnips and inoculate it with the old culture. The food many aquarists give their infusoria cultures consists of condensed milk. A few drops are added to the

Health

culture until the fluid just turns cloudy; add more only when the solution has become almost clear again.

Another excellent rearing food is the larvae of the little brine shrimp, *Artemia salina*. The eggs of this small shrimp can be purchased at all pet shops; breeding instructions (the eggs have to be soaked in salt water if the larvae are to hatch) are usually enclosed.

Fishes that are fond of plant food can be given occasional pieces of lettuce leaf. But remove the leaf again before it starts to rot, or you will have badly fouled water.

There are two basic principles of feeding our fish. The first is to feed as varied a diet as possible. The second is to feed too little rather than too much. Uneaten food decays and fouls the water. Fishes that are always satiated grow inactive and come to suffer from fatty degeneration, one of the most frequent causes of death among aquarium fishes, especially in beginners' tanks. Ideally, our fishes should forever be in search of food. One or two days of fasting per week are a great advantage for fully-grown animals. The fry, however, virtually need to be "standing in food."

Disease

Fishes become ill, too, and often we are at wits' end when an infectious disease breaks out in the aquarium. There are many diseases about which we can do very little. What is true for humans applies to fishes as well: prevention is better than cure. The most reliable prevention is a healthy tank: water with a high oxen content, an aeration that makes the water circulate and drives out excessive carbon dioxide, and above all clean water that still deserves to be called water. If the fishes are left to swim in their own liquid manure, one must not be surprised if they become susceptible to disease. Overfed fishes also seem to be particularly disease prone!

Ich

We do not have the space here to discuss all fish diseases and their possible cures. There is one, however, that we shall mention, since it is common and can destroy all the fishes in the tank within a short period; on the other hand, if noticed in time it can be successfully treated. This is ichthyophtheriasis, or white spot

79

Health

disease. This tongue-twisting word really means "fish louse," but the parasite causing the disease is not a louse but a microscopically small ciliate known as *Ichthyophthirius*. This parasite lives in the skin of fishes and there produces small white nodules immediately recognizable to the naked eyed. The organism multiplies in a special devopmental cycle and its numerous offspring infect the other fishes in the aquarium. If one is not careful, all the fishes will die within a short period. The *Ichthyophthirius* nodules appear to cause a kind of itch in the fish; at least the animals are seen to rub themselves on plants and stones. This is always a suspicious sign, and if we observe such rubbing we should immediately check to see if any of the fishes show a white nodule.

This feared parasite can be controlled with therapeutic agents every pet shop has in stock. Ich is susceptible to treatment only during its active reproductive stage, when tiny larvae are free in the aquarium. The nodules or cysts on the fishes or the bottom of the tank do not respond to treatment. Malachite green, used as directed on the bottle, is effective. Tetras and other fishes sensitive to malachite green should be treated with acriflavine.

The Best Aquarium Book in the World!

This book, the one you are now reading, is published by T.F.H. Publications, Inc., the world's largest publisher of tropical fish books. The "T.F.H." stands for *Tropical Fish Hobbyist®* , the largest circulation monthly aquarium publication. Dr. Herbert R. Axelrod and the staff of T.F.H. have issued a large aquarium book available both in permanent bound form and looseleaf entitled *Exotic Tropical Fishes*. The expanded edition contains over 1,000 color photographs in 1,312 pages. It contains all you have to know about aquarium fishes. See a copy at your pet shop. Free monthly supplements are available in *Tropical Fish Hobbyist®* magazine.

Exotic Tropical Fishes, *the best-selling, most complete aquarium book in the world.*

80